Spirituality

The Top 25 Best Techniques For Becoming Enlightened And At Peace

By Ace McCloud
Copyright © 2015

Disclaimer

The information provided in this book is designed to provide helpful information on the subjects discussed. This book is not meant to be used, nor should it be used, to diagnose or treat any medical condition. For diagnosis or treatment of any medical problem, consult your own physician. The publisher and author are not responsible for any specific health or allergy needs that may require medical supervision and are not liable for any damages or negative consequences from any treatment, action, application or preparation, to any person reading or following the information in this book. Any references included are provided for informational purposes only. Readers should be aware that any websites or links listed in this book may change.

Table of Contents

Introduction 5

Chapter 1: Know Thyself – Awareness, Acceptance and Being Present 8

Chapter 2: Choose a Spiritual Life – Obsessions, the Past and Being Grateful 13

Chapter 3: Spiritual Aids – Tools to Help You Grow Spiritually 16

Chapter 4: Stay Positive, Be Truthful and Don't Judge 23

Chapter 5: Be Inspired by Nature, Arts, Culture and Yes, by Discomfort 27

Chapter 6: Thoughtful Actions – Meditation, Affirmation, and Prayer 35

Chapter 7: Final Stages – Surrender and Patience 43

Conclusion 46

My Other Books and Audio Books 47

Be sure to check out my website for all my Books and Audio books.

www.AcesEbooks.com

Introduction

I want to thank you and congratulate you for buying the book, "Spirituality: The Top 25 Best Techniques For Becoming Enlightened And At Peace."

This book contains proven steps and strategies on how to strengthen the spiritual part of your being, how to seek spiritual enlightenment and how to increase your inner peace.

Spirituality is often confused with religion; people often think that if you are a spiritual person, you must be active in a church, temple, mosque or another religious group. This is not always true. Although religion can be a part of spirituality, it is not a defining point. So, what exactly *is* spirituality? That is a good question. One person may define spirituality as going to church. Another may describe it as being in tune with your own spirit, while others say spirituality is a matter of being present in the moment. Some people think of spirituality as a connection with spirits, those that live on the earth or with the spirits of people who have left the earth for bigger and better things. In this book we define spirituality as the ability to connect to matters of the spirit. A spiritual person might take time to enjoy the beauty of a blooming garden on the way to work, while others scurry on by without even noticing its delightful loveliness. Sensitivity to beauty is but one aspect of spirituality.

Elizabeth Gilbert, author of "Eat, Pray, Love" wrote: "Religion is for those who don't want to go to hell and spirituality is for those who have already been there." If you feel like you have been to hell and back in your life, you have probably emerged from the experience with a heightened awareness of what really matters. Often what matters most will be something spiritual in nature, something as intangible as loving relationships, or as simple as a breeze caressing your face. When we run away from our hellish experiences we tend to gravitate toward something that means more than what we left behind. That pursuit is the essence of spirituality.

The YouTube video Religion Vs Spirituality by Sean Meshorer provides the basics of spirituality and shows some differences between it and the subset of spirituality known as religion.

Spiritual people tend to have an inner glow. They may seem wise beyond their years. As a child, I knew an older gentleman who happened to be very active in his church. He wore a shock of brilliant white hair above twinkling blue eyes and light seemed to radiate from every pore of his body. This man was wise, kind and truly cared about helping others instead of pursuing financial gain and professional power. Amazingly, he always had more than enough money to support his large family, yet he was constantly reaching out to help others in need. Because of his spiritual foundation, this man had more than he needed to not just survive; he lived a happy and generous life.

I have often wished I could be like this man. Now that I am a little older, I realize I can have some of things he had. I have stopped worrying about fame and fortune because I trust that my spiritual Source will take care of my life. I am learning to accept myself, both the bad and the good. I am learning to love the Self I have been given.

It is not easy to follow a spiritual path. People who were brought up in a spiritual household might have an advantage because they grew up surrounded by examples and mentors. Even so, only you can pursue spiritual growth; nobody can do it for you. Although you may be spiritually mature, this doesn't mean you are perfect. Even my godly, white-haired friend didn't function in spiritual mode all the time.

Difficulty seems to invade life almost on cue when things seem to be going well. Your car might break down just after successfully getting a tooth fixed. When things appear to be going well, a child may make a mistake and saddle you with legal problems. You might become sick just after acquiring a new job, so you feel you can't take off time to get better. These difficulties can be a challenge to your spiritual life. The true challenge, as human beings with all our foibles, is to handle these obstacles without losing faith, trusting that our Source will provide for our needs. Instead of destroying us, a challenge can actually strengthen our spirit. We all have an innate, spirituality; the focus of this book is to nurture and strengthen our spirits.

Think about the people you know. I'll bet those who have impacted your life the most are spiritual people. Life is not about you, but it *is* about the people who have touched your life and the manner in which you, in turn, touch others. That, in a nutshell, is spirituality.

There are many components that combine to make up spirituality, but in this book we will focus on a short list of:

- Self-awareness
- Self-acceptance
- Living in the present
- Forgiveness
- Compassion
- Patience
- Surrender
- Gratitude

I have included 25 techniques designed to foster spiritual growth. Pursue the activities that speak to your current needs. These techniques are designed to nurture your spiritual being and free it to flourish.

Pierre Teilhard de Chardin, the priest, philosopher and paleontologist, once said, "We are not human beings having a spiritual experience. We are spiritual beings having a human experience." May your spiritual being prosper!

Chapter 1: Know Thyself – Awareness, Acceptance and Being Present

One of the most important things you can do for yourself is to get to know who you are. This is valuable, whether or not you think of yourself as spiritual.

When you learn to play an instrument, you become consciously aware of where you need to put your fingers in order to make different notes. When you first start learning the instrument, you have to pay close attention to what your fingers are doing in order to play a C note instead of playing an F. Learning to be self-aware is similar to learning an instrument. You must teach yourself to pay attention to your emotions, your actions and your motivations. It is important to pay attention to what you are saying, how you are saying it, and the underlying thoughts that make up your inner dialogue as you choose what to say or do.

When you are self-aware, you are able think before you act. For example, your boss comes in and accuses you of forgetting to send a fax to the corporate office. Your immediate reaction may be to speak up defensively, telling your boss that you *did* send it. However, when you are self-aware, you may be able to simply hand your boss the fax confirmation as evidence that the fax actually did go through.

How does being self-aware help you become more spiritual? Self-awareness allows you to think clearly and act appropriately, because you are fully aware of both your own capabilities and the circumstances that surround you. Because you know yourself, you will be able to act deliberately, not by panic driven knee-jerk reactions. You are calmly confident that you have the skills to express yourself appropriately. Self-awareness allows your spirit to see the whole situation instead of just the immediate provocation. It sets you free to be both objective and understanding of others' spiritual and emotional needs.

It is essential to care for your physical, emotional, mental and spiritual well-being. Take time for yourself. Get enough rest. Give your body and mind good nutrition and do some of the things you enjoy in life like listening to music, watching TV, playing video games, playing sports, reading, gardening, cooking or whatever it is you like to do. It is important to enjoy life if you want to develop your spirituality. A grumpy person does not an enlightened person make. Just be careful not to overdo the things you like at the expense of things that must be done, such as paying the bills.

So, how *do* you come to know yourself? For starters, ask a few friends and acquaintances how they view you. Do they think that you are fun to be around? Do you come across as overly sensitive, or do they have a good time with you? Ask them to tell you about your best and worse qualities. What do they like about you? Ask yourself what are your strengths and weaknesses. Give yourself some time to think about your life; it takes time and practice to become self-aware.

This takes a lot of courage and many people may not like the answers they get. However, if you want to get better, this is a very important exercise that I would highly recommend doing.

Technique #1 - Being Self-Aware
Evaluate yourself. At the top of a sheet of paper, write, "What is my favorite?" On the left side of the paper write the items that follow, giving yourself several lines in which to answer:

- Color
- Activity
- Season
- Food
- Music
- Book
- Movie
- Video Game
- Person

Write down the first thing that comes to mind. (You can always add your second or third choices; that's why you allowed plenty of space!) This should give you a good idea of who you are in daily life.

Now, on another piece of paper, write down your strengths and weaknesses. Write down some of the thoughts that dominate your day and ask yourself:

- What do I believe is true?
- What motivates me to do things?
- What are my most common emotions?
- What would I be willing to die to protect?

Using your answers, write a short story of your life, including only the most important parts. For example, you might include your 16th birthday, your wedding day, the day your children were born, or other important milestones. Writing this little biography will help you become more self-aware.

Another activity that will help you to develop inner peace and self-awareness is to make your own personal vision board. Get a tri-fold science fair board or a large piece of poster board. Look for images and quotes that reflect the person you would like to be. Cut out and attach these images or quotes to your vision board. For example, if you like to cook and would like to do this professionally, you might include the image of a chef on your vision board. If you feel you are here on this earth to heal others, you may choose pictures of medications or surgical tools and write quotes from Mother Theresa or healers who inspire you. Put your vision board where you will see it every day and change it up as often as you like.

This will reinforce your self-awareness and will visually document the progress of your spiritual life.

Technique #2: Accept Yourself and Others

One of the hardest things you can do is to accept who you are. We all have specific strengths and weaknesses; some can be changed, but others can't. It is important to accept the things you cannot change and work around them to better yourself. I am a workaholic, which sometimes works to the detriment of my family. I find it difficult to stop toiling away because the drive to work is ingrained in me. I accept that I will put in long hours at work, but know it is important to actually stop and make time for my family. Once I'm doing something with them, I'm fully immersed and having fun. Getting there is the problem. Since I accept that I have this weakness, I can strategize ways to stop and spend time with my family without causing my work to suffer.

Accepting all of yourself, including your spirituality, helps the pieces of your life fall into place. Conversely, until you accept who you are, you will not be able to give yourself to others wholly.

This works the other direction as well. Once you have accepted yourself in all your wonderful and challenging aspects, it is easier to accept the foibles of others. You will find it less difficult to understand that their weaknesses belong to them and not to you. You will be more able to accept others as they are, letting go completely of any illusion that you are put on this earth to change them. Influence them, yes; but change them, no. That's their job.

Technique #3 – Be Present in the Moment

Brian L. Weiss, psychiatrist and author of <u>Messages from the Masters,</u> studies past and future life regressions and what happens to the soul after death. He once said, "Forgive the past. It is over. Learn from it and let go."

A truly spiritual person is able to meld the past and future into the present. The past is important, looking forward to the future is beneficial, but living in the present is essential.

Living in the present isn't always easy to do, however. If you are 40 years old, you have 40 years of past memories and desires for the future to sort through. Our memories are often distorted by emotions and subsequent events; this can make them somewhat unreliable as time goes by. Memories and wishes are often discussed in that inner dialog going on inside our heads. What is happening as you read this sentence is the present. It is real, not an illusion, as are the past and the future.

Living in the present frees you from the constraints dictated by anxiety about the past or fear of the future. Let's say you are sitting in a dentist's office right now; if you have never been to a dentist before, you are living in the present, experiencing only the normal discomfort faced by those who are entering the unknown, but highly aware of every detail in the room. Those of us who have experienced dental visits in the past may have additional anxiety because we *know* what happens behind that door! This anxiety can easily prevent us from living in the present because our fear is based on actual experience. But, let's say you are able to pull yourself away from how past experience is coloring what you expect to happen in a few minutes. Look around you. If children are present, watch them play. Notice how they are likely not bound up by anxiety, but are probably paying attention to whatever draws their interest at the moment. Can you imitate them and bring yourself fully into contact with the concrete reality that is yours at this moment? Consciously turn your attention to each of your senses. What colors are you seeing? Is the room light and airy or does it feel stifling? What shapes do you see? Focus on the chair you are sitting on; is it soft? Hard? Smooth? Rough? I could go on, but I think you get the idea. Instead of escaping into the world of future dread or past pain, sometimes the present can be a pleasant relief.

Living in the present allows your spiritual self to emerge. Your spiritual being loves and accepts all; it has great compassion. The present self does not judge or form opinions and it pays no attention to the opinions of others. It takes situations as they come and deals with them without fear or presuppositions. The video, All it Takes is 10 Mindful Minutes from ted.com, can help you explore this further. It explains being present and mindful in easy-to-understand terms.

Once in the present, it is easier to be aware of all the beauty in the world, unhindered by past experiences and undisturbed by the "what if's" of the future. All of a sudden the universe looks bigger, yet more connected.

To help you enter into the present, here are a couple exercises you can try. Focusing on one thing alone will help you in remain in the present.

This exercise starts with focusing on how your body moves and what you are doing at the moment:

1. Sit in a comfortable position.

2. Breathe in a normal manner and pay close attention to how you are breathing. Feel your breath as you inhale through your nose and breathe out through your mouth. Notice how your stomach expands as you take a breath and contracts as you exhale. Hold an image of your lungs inflating and deflating every time you breathe. Concentrate on just breathing, without letting your mind wander, for about 5 to 10 minutes. At first you may find this very difficult; after 3 minutes you may think you've been sitting there for about 20. Do not despair; this gets easier with practice. Try it daily for a week, and see if I'm right.

Another method is as follows:

1. Sit comfortably, but not so comfortably as to fall asleep.

2. Let your mind wander wherever it wishes for a few minutes, then slowly and deliberately start to focus on exactly what is happening around you.

3. Are the birds chirping? Did the furnace just switch on? Can you hear the TV in another room? Take notice of everything you sense, including listening, seeing, smelling, hearing and feeling. You are in the present.

As you can see, being in the present isn't all that easy and requires practice. It is impossible to always live in the present. In fact, it can sometimes help your spirituality to remember the past and plan for the future. The biggest thing to remember is that those who live in the present tend not to judge. They take things as they come.

Watch how babies look at and react to the world. They have few to no preconceptions and have really no sense of future or past. They exist in the present. They listen for their parents' voices, cry when they're hungry or wet, and interact with others who are right in front of them. We all start out by living in the present, but somewhere along the line our minds become filled with experiences that kick us out of the present; we then gravitate toward a preoccupation with the past or a focus on the future.

One of the best ways that I have found to stay in the present is to use the "Mindfulness Meditation" audio from Hypnosis Downloads. It is really great and will definitely help you to stay in the present. Try using it just once a day and see what a difference you experience.

Chapter 2: Choose a Spiritual Life – Obsessions, the Past and Being Grateful

Spirituality doesn't just happen. You don't just wake up one day with a fully-formed spirit. No, spirituality is a conscious choice. It is a conscious, *daily* choice, requiring constant reminders and the development of habits that the ancients called "spiritual disciplines." The techniques in this book can help you develop habits or disciplines that will nourish the various aspects of your spiritual life.

Each aspect of spirituality must be present in your life if you are going to actually be spiritual. You will have a hard time finding inner peace if you do not have compassion or love for others. You cannot be truly spiritual if you are filled with negative attitudes; negativity will put a real damper on your inspiration.

Neither is it appropriate to say you are being spiritual if you only practice one or two aspects of spirituality and ignore glaring weaknesses in other areas. You may say, "Okay, I'll be compassionate on Tuesday. I'll accept myself on Wednesday, but I'll skip Thursday because I have to work late. On Friday I think I'll live in the present." It just doesn't work that way. Just like being good at most things, it takes diligence and practice every day.

Technique #4 – Avoid Obsessing

Spirituality is a matter of life balance. Obsessions are a form of unbalance and are rarely helpful. Even obsessing over something positive like spirituality is not a good thing. Hunting down inner peace with all guns a-blazing is not the way to catch it. The harder you battle for peace, the more it will elude your grasp.

You may be anxious about your daughter's dating, but obsessing over it can ruin your normally calm demeanor and jeopardize an already tenuous relationship. You may find yourself doing and saying things that alienate yourself from the daughter you only want to protect. If you want to lose weight, you can obsess about it all you want, but your worry is what causes your body to dump chemicals into your system that actually prevent you from knocking off those unwanted pounds. Likewise, you cannot fill yourself with inner peace by obsessing over it.

So, how do you know if you have an obsession? This is an important question because we tend to be unaware of our own obsessions. Take a look around you. Do you have pictures, statues or other items that relate to one person, place, or thing? It is okay to have family photos in your home or office, but when you start covering every space on your wall with your daughter's photos, when every activity you do centers around her and the only person you do anything with is her, you may have an unhealthy obsession. Even if you haven't been able to identify any obsessions in your life, ask a friend if they have noticed any obsessive behaviors on your part. Friends may bring something to light that you are completely unaware of. If your friends don't have any suggestions, you are likely in the clear on this issue. (Phew! Heave a sigh of relief!)

Your spiritual objective is to be able to act from a position of compassion, positive thinking, gratefulness, and inspiration without being completely preoccupied by it. Choosing to put obsessions behind you is one step toward becoming a more spiritual person.

Technique #5 – Remember the Past (within reason)

I know we said living in the present is essential to gain spirituality, but remembering the past (not living in it), is also beneficial. It is important for the spiritual person to remember things that happened in the past. Some believe that humans are born as spiritual beings, we just forget easily. Remembering your past may trigger old spiritual tendencies, reawakening them into existence.

Pull out all those old photo albums you have sitting on the bookshelves or in closets. Go through them alone or with your family. Maybe you have felt your spirituality slipping lately. You were a spiritual person before, but situations and time have made you less so. You want to regain the spiritual presence in your life. Old photos of the past can remind you of things you did and people you knew when your spirituality was at its apex.

Regardless of your personal history of spirituality, you may be able to use old photos to spark your memory of spiritual people you have known in the past. A friend of mine had a grandmother who was a saint. She helped many people in her community. If they were sick, she brought their family food. If someone died, she was there to comfort those left behind, and – again – to bring food. She fed the poor, clothed them, befriended them and never asked for anything in return. My friend was reminded of her grandmother's accomplishments as she browsed through an old family scrapbook. She became a more spiritual person by reminding herself of her grandmother's example, letting it mold who she wanted to become. I hope you will be able to remember at least one person who can serve, even posthumously, as a spiritual mentor. If not, there are many people in the past or present you can choose to model.

Technique #6 – Gratitude

A spiritual person is grateful for what they have. The ability to see all the wonderful things you have been given will help you become a more spiritual person. It is easy to get used to what we have, as if these things are our right, and forget that they came to us from somewhere else, from someone else. This awareness does not come naturally; you have to consciously choose to see all the great things you have in your life.

I have built the practice of gratitude into my morning ritual. When I first wake up, right after I have chosen to stretch my face into a smile, I think of three things that I am grateful for. When I jumpstart this "attitude of gratitude" first thing in the morning, I find I am primed to notice things I am grateful for throughout the day. I even find myself thanking other people for their kindnesses. I invite you to try adding this to your morning routine for a month and see if you notice any changes in your life.

Be grateful for all the good things that come to you through your quest for spirituality. I often make it a habit to call friends who might feel under the weather physically or emotionally, just to let them know they are not alone and that I care. Recently I came down with a bad cold and missed a few regularly scheduled activities. Several people called me just to see if I was okay. I felt grateful to those people and that warm, fuzzy feeling inside helped my spirituality grow and stay strong.

If you are grateful for your job, you are more likely to go the extra mile to do a good job. That reflects positively on you and may lead to greater success. If you are grateful for your family and friends, you are more likely to be an inspiration to them and allow them to inspire you. Life is always better when the people around you get along and swiftly resolve their conflicts. This is the perfect atmosphere in which to foster your spirituality.

Another exercise you may find useful is to write down all the things for which you are grateful for in your life. You can make a poster of who and what you are grateful for, gluing on a paper some photos of people who inspire you or pictures that represent things you are grateful for. Hang this gratitude board somewhere you will see it frequently and be reminded to choose to be grateful for the abundance in your life.

In order to be grateful, a spiritual person must first know how to forgive. Forgiveness frees you from the chains of past events that bog you down in a morass of regret, shame, anger and bitterness, preventing you from growing and moving forward in life. If you find it difficult to be thankful, you may want to first address any past wrongs that are holding you back. After you have forgiven you others and pursued forgiveness for wrongs you may have done (especially forgiving your Self).

Chapter 3: Spiritual Aids – Tools to Help You Grow Spiritually

Becoming spiritual can take a great deal of work. This process can be facilitated by observing and learning how others go about growing spiritually. Reading and studying can help your mind absorb unfamiliar ideas. This chapter also focuses on building love and compassion as a way to grow spiritually. Helping others is a natural outgrowth of love and compassion for them. Journaling will help you identify your spiritual progress over time.

Technique #7 – Observe

For some people it is easy to be the center of attention, but not so easy to take a backseat and just observe. If you are one of these people, you may want to put aside all of that charisma for a while and teach yourself to sit back and listen, look and enjoy. On the other hand, if you are already able to stand to the side and calmly observe everything around you, take advantage of this skill and use your observational powers to learn from those around you.

Sometimes people get caught up in leading and being the center of attention. A spiritual person is often a leader, but knows it is more important to perceive their surroundings and pay attention to the emotions and the words of others. My best friend in elementary school was very introverted and painfully shy. He didn't talk much; he didn't have to because I knew what he was thinking, so I talked enough for the both of us! Kyle was a good artist, even at the age of 8. Because of his shyness, he was often overlooked by others. Our third grade teacher was a wonderful middle-aged woman who just glowed with spirituality. She was kind, gentle and always knew what was going on in her classroom. When she chose samples of our learning to post on the wall of the classroom for parents' day, she could have easily overlooked Kyle and opted to post Marla's lovely handwriting or all the book reports Matthew had written since school started. However, she had noticed Kyle's little doodles that covered his notebook. Because she had paid attention to the quietest of her students, this wonderful teacher asked Kyle to create a collage of small drawings, which she placed in the very center of the bulletin board. The other students' achievements were arranged around this marvelous centerpiece.

The teacher's spirituality allowed her to notice Kyle and impact the life of a lowly kid in the classroom by helping him outgrow his shyness. Ultimately, Kyle became a prominent figure in the contemporary art world. To this day, Kyle is the first to acknowledge the impact this teacher's spirituality made in his life.

If you tend to be driven and find it difficult to stop and observe, set aside several times a day for a few minutes of focused observation. Right before or after lunch, or early in the morning, can each be prime times for people watching. Set aside time in the evening to observe your family. You will be surprised at the spiritual awareness you will gain merely by observing family, friends, or co-workers. Do not judge what they are doing or saying, just watch and listen in order to better understand them.

Plants and animals are also useful subjects for your observation. Take your dog for a walk and pay attention to the leaves on the trees, the flowers in the yards you pass, and to the outside smells. Pay attention to the things your dog notices; you might even want to try to see the world from his viewpoint for a change!

Observation can increase your appreciation of life and all the people, places and things in it. It tends to foster spiritual growth through the appreciation of the beauty that surrounds you.

Technique #8 – Read and Study

A good way to become more spiritual is to read and study about spiritual people or spiritual situations. You don't have to read religious texts like the Bible, the Bhagavad Gita, the Koran or the Torah, but this doesn't hurt. My brother-in-law, whom I consider a very spiritual person, is a Christian, but he has read and studied almost every religious text available from all the major religions. Jonathan feels that what he has discovered has helped strengthen his faith and has sharpened his understanding of God. He has discerned similarities between Christianity and other religions; his inner peace has grown as he has identified interconnections between the different faiths. Jonathan believes that God is God, no matter what name you give him. He can appreciate Buddha as he does Jesus Christ and he does not judge anyone because of their beliefs, or lack thereof. Studying all these religious texts has enhanced his spirituality.

As I mentioned before, you do not have to limit yourself to religious texts. If you do a search under spirituality, you will find thousands of books, from the writings of Neale Donald Walsch in his <u>Conversations with God</u> to James Redfield's <u>Celestine Prophecy</u>. You will find many books written by the current Dalai Llama XIV and by Deepak Chopra, a motivational speaker and author.

You can even choose from religious fiction. The <u>Left Behind</u> collection by Tim LaHaye and Jerry Jenkins and the Amish series by Beverly Lewis come to mind. There is even a spiritual book about the lowly sea bird by Richard Bach. It is aptly entitled <u>Jonathan Livingston Seagull</u>.

You can find all kinds of self-help books about and by spiritual people such as Henri Nouwen, Charles Williams, or Elie Wiesel, a political activist and professor who was a prisoner at Auschwitz. Don't forget works about Celtic religious mythology by Joseph Campbell and Caitlin Matthews.

<u>Self-help</u> books can also be very helpful. The book you are reading right now is one example among quite a few that I have written. Don't stop here. See what

other books I have as well as other authors. Many of the most enlightened people on this planet make a habit of reading good literature every day.

The more you read and study, the more your mind can be infused with ideas that support your spiritual life. Set aside time each day for reading and study and stick to it. Choose the time that works best for you; if you are an early riser you may prefer to read in the morning, or you may prefer a lunchtime infusion to break up your busy workday. Some people prefer reading right before they go to bed at night.

Don't forget about [audio books](). You can listen to them on your commute or while you exercise or cook dinner. Reading and study are essential tools to help you grow spiritually. I have a nice array of audio books you can listen to if that is your thing.

Technique #9 – Love

Those who give and receive love on a regular basis are generally able to connect with inner peace and spirituality more easily than those who do not. The love I am speaking about is not sexual love, although there is nothing wrong with using physical intimacy to enhance your inner peace. In this case, however, I am speaking primarily about love for family, friends, and a general love for humanity. Harmony in the home and in your daily interaction will reduce your stress and can consequently increase your happiness. Loving your friends can provide an emotional foundation upon which your spirituality may grow and flourish. The more intimate a friendship, the greater potential it holds for nourishing your spirit, and theirs.

Almost every religion stresses that you should love, regardless of a person's race, gender, culture, or personality. Those who give money to a charity are exhibiting a general love for humankind. They love enough to share what they have with those who are less fortunate. When you are generous with your love, it encourages your spirit to grow. You can donate to a charity, help a less fortunate family by providing some basic needs, or volunteer at a senior living center, animal shelter, or soup kitchen. You can visit a sick or elderly friend or share your talents with an organization like your church, a little league baseball team, the Boy Scouts, Girl Scouts or 4-H. If you can knit, you can knit mittens, scarves, or hats and take them to homeless shelters. Perhaps you are a wonderful cook. You can use your special gifting to provide dinners to elderly people who would normally be eating a sandwich instead of enjoying your delicious hot meal. Use your talents and the things you enjoy doing in order to serve others. Loving from the heart is what builds your spirit.

A good way to foster love in your heart is to choose a person you do not like and make a focused attempt to be kind and generous to them. Who knows? You may find out they aren't as bad as you thought they were. No matter what, you will be spiritually boosted because you have chosen one more person to love.

Technique # 10 – Develop Compassion

A quote from Paul Rezendes says, "Compassion . . . is an understanding of the unity of all things. It is an awareness that I is not separate from thou, that whatever is happening to the planet, or to another person, is happening to me. Compassion is total empathy, an absolute sense of connection."

Compassion is a trait everyone should strive to achieve. Compassion is feeling for a person in the midst of their predicament. You may feel compassion for your friend who lost her spouse or for a little girl whose dog ran away.

Compassion is much stronger when you have been in the same position as the person who is hurting. We call this empathy, the ability to share the feeling of another. If you have lost your spouse, you will feel more deeply for your friend who just lost his wife. If you ever had a pet run away, you will feel more sadness for the child who lost her dog.

However, personal experience is not a prerequisite for having compassion. You can still feel sympathy, sadness and worry for your friend who just became a widower even if your spouse is still alive and well. In fact, if you are any type of good person, it is hard *not* to be moved by the pain of others.

Compassion is a big part of what makes us human. You can express your compassion through kind words, thoughtful advice (when requested), meeting material needs, and by listening actively (not just tossing in an "uh-huh" while your mind wanders).

Technique # 11 – Help Others

Helping others goes hand in hand with fostering compassion. Lending a helping hand increases spirituality and inner peace. Spiritual people often perform selfless acts. They are able to respond to the needs of others because they have the inner spiritual strength to look beyond their own needs.

Helping others is what connects you to the human race. When you get outside yourself and see life through the eyes of another person, you have become both more human and more spiritual. Helping others also feels good and - just like the old Grinch - your heart will grow three times larger when you help someone else.

Opportunities for helping others abound today. Volunteering is a good way to help others. Just visiting a rest home and playing bingo with the residents helps boost their spirits and feeds yours as well. If you play the piano, guitar, or accordion, facilitate a sing-a-long. Most of the residents love it if you sing songs from their era.

Offer to babysit for the single mother next door who is raising toddler twins and looks rather stressed. By offering her a few hours of time to herself you can help her feel refreshed and re-energized.

Check the internet for volunteer opportunities in your community. You will have many from which to choose and all will give you a satisfied soul while providing relief to another person by meeting practical needs. Most American cities provide a clearinghouse of volunteering opportunities by dialing 411 on your phone.

Technique #12 – Keep a Spiritual Journal

I have been a journal fanatic for years. Journaling helps me both with my writing career and with my life. I use it to practice writing almost every day and from my journal I frequently get great ideas for more writing projects. My journal helps me focus and it helps me remember things. Journaling has also helped to build my inner peace, because it gives me a way to process events or problems I need to work through.

To start journaling, you will need a notebook of some kind. Spiral notebooks are acceptable, but I like to purchase bound journals; they look like real books so they feel special. Call me silly, but I am more apt to journal each night simply because my journal looks elegant! The main drawback to spiral notebooks is that they tend to lose pages. Not only do the bound journals keep their pages and look good, but the pages themselves are made of higher quality paper. This means they stay flexible and last much longer without yellowing. I even use a special pen to journal. At first I used a calligraphy pen (talk about having a special experience!), but I've found that gel pens can be every bit as elegant. Besides, they don't smudge and the ink remains dark much longer than with a regular ink pen.

If you wish, you can keep a digital journal. Just create a word processing document on your computer and type in it every night. You can also use a great program called OneNote to make a very handy digital journal. However, I personally find there is something special about handwritten work that makes it more intimate. It seems to evoke more vivid memories and spark deeper emotions than the somewhat antiseptic environment of the digital page.

Set aside a specific time each day for your journaling. Morning might be a good time as long as you aren't rushing around, trying to get ready for work or get the kids off to school. If the only real time you have is during your lunch hour that is fine, too. Alternately, you may prefer to journal at night after the kids are tucked in bed and you have some peaceful time to yourself. Just pick a time that works for you and try to keep that time set apart for journaling. You can also check out a very popular book right now called the 5 minute journal. I started using this in the mornings and it is a great way to start the day!

There is no hard and fast rule for what to write in your journal. A journal can serve as a brain dump; just getting things down on paper can help remove some of the miscellany that clutters your mind and distracts your thinking. You can use your journal to process your emotions; many people find the act of writing helps them evaluate what has happened recently. It is possible to write down painful events as an act of creating closure, enabling you to set them aside and move forward. Writing down choices you have made, goals you are choosing to pursue, or changes you have decided to make helps to make your commitment real. You are more likely to follow up on your decisions if you put them down in black and white (or whatever color you choose; I prefer purple or green, myself).

It is also possible that journaling can help depression, as recent research has suggested that worrying too much leads to over dreaming which in turn leads to you not getting enough quality sleep, which in turn leaves you waking up exhausted and tired. The best video on this I have ever seen is from Uncommon Knowledge and it details the [Depression Learning Path](#).

If you draw a blank when it comes time to write, just start writing whatever is on your mind. You may be surprised at what comes out.

Here are some additional ideas if you need a jumpstart in your journaling:

- What you did today
- Ways you helped others, acts of compassion, gifts of love
- Important observations about life in general
- What you are worried or anxious about
- Plans you want to implement in the future
- Progress toward your goals (including your goal of being more spiritual)
- Surprises, both good and bad
- Funny things people said or did
- Emotions you experienced and what triggered them

You can include anything you like in your journal, from pet peeves to recipes to illustrations.

To get the most out of your journaling, I also highly recommend reviewing your past entries on a regular basis. You do not write in a journal and lock it away so nothing is ever seen again. The writing itself can be cathartic, but reflecting on those pages after some time has passed can give you even more insight. You may laugh, cry and experience a whole host of emotions as you connect with the self you were then. While you may sometimes wonder why you wrote down the things you're reading, your nonjudgmental acceptance of your own thoughts and feelings from that time can serve as a powerful affirmation of your Self. This type of reflection can also promote inner peace, especially if you can see progress you are making toward a personal goal.

You don't have to reflect on the entire journal every time you open it. I suggest placing a bookmark, starting with an entry from a few months up to a year prior to the present. Your reflection on these entries may give you a different perspective on situations that you lacked earlier, simply because you were right on top of the situation when you were writing. A little time can provide fresh insight into your entry. Your additional experiences since that time may have totally altered your opinions.

For example, you may have written an entry in January, describing how angry you felt toward your best friend, because you needed help and she did not have time for you. You thought she was selfish and you swore the next time she needed help you would not be there for her. One year later you may reflect on this situation from a completely different perspective. Now you know that January was the time your friend learned her mother was dying of cancer and you didn't know it yet. Your reflection is able to bring feelings of compassion to bear on the situation. Since that time, your friend's mother has died. What you know now may spur you on to apologize for any harsh words or attitudes you may have communicated. You could be motivated do something kind to make up for all those nasty thoughts you had at the time. Or you may be reminded that she is still grieving, so you choose to reach out and provide her what comfort you can. If you want help knowing how to comfort a grieving friend, let me recommend <u>The Dave Test</u>, by Frederick W. Schmidt. Any kind response may bring you closer to inner peace and spirituality.

Chapter 4: Stay Positive, Be Truthful and Don't Judge

Having a positive attitude, telling the truth and avoidance of judgment will help any person become wise and spiritual.

Technique # 13 – Stay Positive

It is so much easier to be spiritual if you are a positive, happy person. Most children begin life with a happy outlook. All the negativity begins to slip in after they start to have bad experiences. Because of these bad experiences, children may begin to shy away from people, places or events that trigger negative emotions or painful associations.

Some people have no problem being positive, but many others find it necessary to consciously choose to look at life from an optimistic or hopeful framework. It is hard to be spiritual if all you have are negative thoughts. People who have spirituality well in hand can be some of the most positive people around. So, how do you change your negativity to a positive perspective? Here are a few suggestions that may help.

Make a list of what you think will help you be positive. Maybe you worry about money and believe making more money will change your mindset. You may think that a bigger house will help you to be happy or give you more opportunities to socialize with friends.

After you have identified what will help you to think positively, try setting some goals that will help you to get there. From the examples above, you can figure out how to make a little more money by taking another job or by selling crafts to save for a larger apartment. To get back in touch with that old friend, try the internet; you can locate almost anyone with an internet search. Once you have discovered where your old friend is living, take the initiative to make the first contact. Since you're planning to move anyhow, consider the possibility of relocating closer to your friend's home or favorite place. Who knows? Your old friend might miss you, too.

Make a list of the good things that have happened to you. When negativity starts to seep into your life, stop it dead by whipping out your "good things" list and reviewing the positive side of your life.

Technique #14 – Be Truthful

Spiritual people do not have anything to be guilty about; they have no reason not to be truthful.

Several different types of falsehoods exist. One type of untruthfulness is often used to save someone's feelings. We call them "little white lies" and, by and large, our culture excuses them because they are accomplishing a greater good. Perhaps you think your daughter's shaved head looks ridiculous, but you smile and say it looks "different", even though you hate it. In this case you aren't lying; you are just choosing not to reveal everything in your mind. A white lie would be to tell your daughter you like her new look when in reality you detest it. Both statements accomplish the same immediate purpose: you don't want your daughter to react by growing her hair out and dyeing it green, just to get back at you. You speak so as to spare her feelings and – hopefully – to discourage further experimentation.

Here's the deal. White lies are still lies. Even if nobody else knows it, *you* know you are not being truthful, not with yourself and certainly not with the other person. Since any type of falsehood is destructive to your spirit, it's best to avoid white lies in the first place; all it takes is a little creativity. Most people will accept a statement that answers their question, even if it does not reveal every detail of your opinion. Your conscience will be clean and your friend will be content.

Other falsehoods are just plain lies. Let's say you go to the store and spend more money than you have decided is right for your current budget. If you come home, hide your extra purchases and tell your spouse that you only spent the budgeted amount, you are lying through your teeth. You are damaging your spirit and are wounding your conscience. If you do this habitually, you may prevent yourself from making additional spiritual progress. After all, truthfulness is one of the components of a spiritual person.

It can take a lot of guts to be truthful. It is human nature to fabricate falsehoods in order to make ourselves look better in someone else's eyes. However, a truly spiritual person doesn't need to fabricate anything in order to look good; after all, self-acceptance includes accepting the part of us we would rather other people didn't know about. Being truthful can sometimes hurt our lives, even our reputations. Speaking the truth might lead to problems in the short term, but in the long run your truthfulness may show that you are indeed trustworthy. If you tell your daughter you dislike seeing her scalp and that her lack of hair looks horrible, she may rant and rave for a while, but she will appreciate your truthfulness later in life. If you lie, she will likely know it anyhow and will wonder how many other things you have lied about.

Have the courage to be truthful and your spiritual life will not be hindered.

Technique #15 – Avoid Judgment

Somewhere along the line, we learn to be judgmental. Our parents may have modeled this behavior. It may have been reinforced by the words and attitudes of our peers. Whatever the cause, by the time we are adults, we have most likely been wounded by others' judgments of us, and we have learned to pass the judgment on to other people. It's a funny thing; little children do not judge. They may be instinctively selfish, they may say things they have heard others say without knowing the true meaning, but when they are little, children rarely know what it is to judge or criticize others. They accept people at face value and that is that.

Children have to be taught to discern safe people from unsafe people. This is not necessarily judgment; it is an essential protection in today's culture. However, parents can plant the seeds of judgment in their children's minds by melding a healthy discernment with unhealthy condemnation. For example, to teach your child to never open the door to a stranger is healthy discernment; however, if you add that people with a certain skin color or a certain way of talking are despicable, you have crossed the line into judgment. Children can be taught to follow your instructions without adding fear or hatred as a motivation.

Judgment can inhibit your spirituality in profound ways. People who judge are not living in the present. Their focus is blurred by a tendency to fill their minds with "what ifs," For example, the Arab man sitting across from you might be a very nice person. However, if you have been put in fear of people who are different, you won't be thinking, "Here is a pleasant looking, kindly man in front of me; he's probably a friend of my Arab neighbor." No, you will likely be influenced by news reports and instead may be thinking one word: "terrorist."

Judging others makes one fearful, angry and unpleasant, which in turn may generate even more fear, anger and unpleasantness. The person who is pursuing spirituality is able to stop this downward spiral and choose to give others the benefit of the doubt. You can actually choose to treat everyone as if they are good until they prove themselves otherwise.

If you judge someone unreasonably, you may miss out on the benefits of what could be a hugely enriching relationship. That Arab sitting across from you could easily share your passion for jazz music. If you judge him out of hand, just think of all the delightful conversations and shared concerts you would of missed out on!

People tend to live up to your expectations of them. Think of the example of trust given to Jean Valjean in *Les Miserables*. One man was rendered an honest citizen by the totally unwarranted trust given to him by a simple cleric who refused to label him a thief. Of course, this requires a considerable risk on your part. Any person you allow into your house could turn out to be a thief; you may well lose your cutlery to a desperate Jean Valjean. But there are risks that are worth taking. Yes, listen to your gut when it tells you to run; just don't let your fear shut you off from society in general. If you do so you end up stifling your spirit and not really living at all.

Judgmental people tend to not be well liked. Nobody wants to be constantly barraged by critical, judgmental speech; no matter *how* justified you may consider your comments. A judgmental person tends to rationalize his slash-and-burn language in the interest of defending the Truth, at least what their idea of what truth is. Never mind the trail of emotionally hemorrhaging victims and the pile of destroyed reputations they may leave behind. The Truth is all that matters to some people. People tend to shy away from a judgmental person for fear they will be judged unreasonably. In my opinion, judgmentalism is the greatest danger to the spirit of people, second only to apathy.

Learn a little more on how to be less judgmental with Mike Freeman's YouTube video, [I'm Right, You're an Idiot -How To Be Less Judgemental-Mike's Nugget #007](#).

Not only do spiritual people not judge others, they do not condemn themselves. Did you know that any time you think or say anything negative, critical, or judgmental about someone else, it is the same as speaking it to yourself? Psychiatrists will tell you that the deepest part of our brain, the part of us that only knows the rudimentary impulses of safe, unsafe, food, and sex, cannot tell the difference between what we tell ourselves and what we tell other people. To this "reptilian brain", as they call it, when you judge or criticize another person, you are in essence judging or criticizing yourself. This deepest part of yourself is very close to your spirit. Wound it, and you can wound your spirituality.

Buddha is credited with the quote, "Do not judge yourself harshly. Without mercy for ourselves we cannot love the world." It is critical that we learn to forgive ourselves. Everyone makes mistakes. When you do, simply accept your mistake as part of being human, take responsibility for any damage you have done, and make restitution to the best of your ability. Do not beat yourself up. Do not try to make yourself feel lower than a snake's belly. Instead, embrace the part of you that is hurting because of your failure. Accept the part of you that made the mistake; acknowledge that you have a weakness and love yourself in that weakness. Only then will you be able to "love the world."

It is perfectly fine to review what went wrong in order to avoid making the same mistake again, but do so *after* you have accepted yourself and forgiven yourself for failing. It is important that you also consciously let the experience go at some point. Otherwise, you will be tempted to get bogged down by brooding on it. Acknowledge your mistake, learn from it, and move on. Let that be it.

Forgive yourself, allow others their humanity too, and choose to "speak the truth in love", as the ancient Christians taught and lived. Your thoughts will stay positive and you will nourish your spirituality.

Chapter 5: Be Inspired by Nature, Arts, Culture and Yes, by Discomfort

Being inspired can give a real boost to your spirituality. Sometimes gazing at an incredible sunset can inspire and put you more in tune with your spiritual side. Some ways to become inspired are:

- Read materials that are uplifting
- Listen to music that is positive
- Foster relationships with positive people who share your interests

Inspiration should feel good, taste sweet and fill your heart with warmth and joy. There are many ways to gain inspiration, such as taking a walk in nature and watching the sun go down over the ocean. Reading inspirational books can help to heal any bad feelings you may have; they are designed to feed your spirituality. Joyful music comes in many forms. Maybe you enjoy Praise and Worship music or prefer to listen to a lively symphony, watch a ballet or attend an opera. Popular music may be just the thing to inspire you. Maybe you enjoy New Age Music or perhaps Heavy Metal speaks to you. Music can make you laugh or cry, but it always can inspire.

It can also be inspirational to spend time with other spiritual people who share your interests and values. A knitting circle may inspire you to try a new scarf pattern. Your book club might inspire you to write a book of your own. If you enjoy playing video games, gathering with other gamers to discuss methods and strategies can be very inspiring.

For more help becoming inspired, please check into my book entitled Inspiration: Harnessing the Power of Inspiration for True Greatness.

Technique # 16 – Let Nature be your Inspiration

Morihel Ueshiba, founder of the Japanese martial art of aikido, said, "Now and again it is necessary to seclude yourself among deep mountains and hidden valleys to restore your link to the source of life." This technique encourages you to draw energy, ideas and spiritual refreshment from the natural things around you.

Absorb each changing hue of a technicolor sky as the sun sets. Gaze at the ancient grandeur of a mighty redwood. Stroll down a woodland trail. Sit beside a quiet stream or soak in the peace of a lake. What you experience here are things not made by man; each one is an intricate act of beauty. Watch a tree bud out in the spring and look closely at the velveteen petals of a rosebud as they unfold. It is easy to believe some spirit is behind their development; these things are too complex, too "other" to have come from a purely human source. I don't understand how anyone can deny the existence of an Ultimate Source after spending time absorbing nature.

Many shamanistic cultures believe that everything contains a spirit, from trees, animals and humans down to the lowliest rock. One type of rock, for example, looks completely nondescript on the outside, but when cut open it is full of crystals. This rock, a geode, holds an entire vibrant universe within its easily overlooked package. Considering this, I can readily understand how the shamans believe that created things house spirits.

Open your eyes to the beauty that exists in your own backyard. There are natural wonders to enjoy everywhere. Rejoice in the Source that brought them into being and let their wholeness infuse you with inner peace. A great time to do this is during spring after a cold winter.

Technique # 17 – Be Inspired by the Arts

The arts have their genesis in creativity. Creativity utilizes the part of the brain that controls imagination, color identification and spatial recognition. Although there is some controversy about how the brain dictates creativity, it is certain that without the use of this portion of the brain, artists would not be able to figure out what colors to use to paint a landscape or how much space they can use to dance without falling off the stage.

Music, visual art, dance and creative writing are all inspired by what has been labeled the right brain. Brain and spirit work together in creative endeavors. Many artists consider their work to be largely a spiritual activity. Even if they deny the spirituality of their work, anyone who creates is echoing the creative work of the Source from whence they originated.

Learning to play an instrument requires focus, thus it encourages living in the present moment. It also encourages body awareness. Playing an instrument requires you to use different parts of your body; most instrumentalists utilize the fingers of both hands, some need the use of their mouth and their physical airway. All instruments require proper breath control, even if what you are playing does not require your breath to make a sound. While we think of our breath as coming from our lungs, it is in reality a conduit from the spirit.

One of my friends plays several instruments as part of her Christian practice of worship. She has explained that there is an aspect of her being that can only 'speak' through the medium of the guitar, while another part of her is expressed most fluently through her cello, and a third aspect is best articulated by her voice. She may be distressed by life events, but when she enters into playing music, especially in a group with other musicians, the stress and anxiety fall away and she is able to regain spiritual wholeness and balance.

Drawing also can help a person become more spiritually focused as they translates what they sees with their eyes to the mind's eye and then onto on the chosen artistic medium. A dancer has to know not only where to put her feet and hands and how to move her body, but also is required to express what is deep within. As a sculptor displaces space through his work, so a dancer uses her body to displace space, with the added dimensions of time and sound, the constraints of expressing one's spirit within the confines of music.

The creative writer has to dig deep within themselves to find a story to be told. The *way* they expresses this story is a function of the spirit.

The person wishing to gain spirituality does not have to physically participate in creating art. You may find great benefit and enjoyment as you absorb it through your eyes and ears. When was the last time a piece of music moved you to tears? When were you last arrested by the beauty of a painting, the intricacies of a sculpture or the wonder of a photo? When did a dance make you want to get up and do the same thing, even though you knew you couldn't make great leaps into the air? Do you remember the last novel you read that brought tears to your eyes or made you laugh? All these emanate from your spirit. Your response to the creativity of others is an act of spiritual resonance. The arts can feed your inner peace, whether you create the art yourself or are simply responding to the beauty created by others.

Technique #18 – Be Inspired by Cultural Practices

<u>*Labyrinths*</u>

Walking a labyrinth is an ancient form of spiritual journey. It quiets the mind, encouraging focus on the present as you walk in the labyrinth. A labyrinth walk connects the body to the mind and the mind to the spirit. Many people find walking in a labyrinth is an unexpected boost to their spiritual peace. A labyrinth reflects the journey into the depths of self and the subsequent return to the world of everyday life.

Do not confuse a maze with a labyrinth; they are two different things. Mazes twist, turn and include dead ends here and there, forcing you to retrace your steps until you find the correct way to the center. A labyrinth contains only one path, which you follow to reach the center and then travel it on the way back out. Walking a labyrinth can feed your spirit as you respond to the imagery within. Upon entering, the walker merely concentrates on the walking. There is no right or wrong way to walk a labyrinth. You can go directly to the center and back out in a few minutes, or you may take your time and inspect each element it includes.

Evidence of labyrinths has been found dating back five millennia. The use of labyrinths spans several cultures, from ancient Greece, to the American Indian medicine wheel, to the intricate representations of the Celtic knot. Labyrinth representations have been found in jewelry, pottery and are even embossed in the floors of holy places.

A Labyrinth is a sequence of concentric circles called circuits. While a number of forms exist, the most common are the three-circuit and the seven-circuit labyrinth. Each labyrinth walk consists of three stages. The first allows the walker to put off the everyday world through the inward passage. Next is the bestowing of peace and spiritual awareness while you are in the center. The final stage consists of walking back out of the labyrinth, taking with you what you received within.

Some labyrinths are just plain dirt or gravel paths in a lawn; some are painted or taped to a floor. I once made a labyrinth using duct tape on the floor. I've also made one in a garden, with the entrance at the foot of a rock-lined babbling stream. In the center of the labyrinth is an old gnarled oak. I created several focal points along the way; these give the visitor space to pause and ponder. One stop contains a sandy Zen garden with rakes and pebbles provided. At another stop a chair invites one to pause and watch birds visit a nearby birdbath and feeder. Another stop consists of a sundial near flowers that are known to attract butterflies. The final stop before reaching the center is a bench containing a box in which are contained inspirational quotes.

Crystals

Some people find that crystals assist their spirituality and provide inner healing. Crystals are living geometric formations created within the earth. The earth contains energy, so it is only logical that crystals retain some of that energy. Each crystal vibrates at a specific frequency. This vibration is thought to have the ability to heal and calm body, mind and spirit. The most effective types of crystals are raw and unfinished, but polished crystals are also used.

People utilize crystals in a variety of ways. Some place a cluster of crystals in their home or office. Others wear crystals as jewelry or carry them in a pocket. Some choose to hold a crystal while meditating or praying.

The theory behind crystal use is that both the body and the crystal – indeed, all things - vibrate. When they are in tune with each other (when they vibrate in the same or in complementary frequencies), the crystal's energy is greatly amplified, which in turn energizes the body. Different crystals have vibrational frequencies that speak to different parts of the body. For example, agates are used to ground the body and spirit. Aquamarine is used to provide clarity of mind, calcite is good for understanding, citrine for joy and abundance, fluorite for balance, garnet for compassion, hematite to dispel negativity, jade for wisdom and peace, lapis lazuli for creative power, malachite to clear energy blockages, obsidian for protection, and rose quartz for balance. Selenite is said to connect you to a higher self. Amethyst is called the peace stone; just placing this gem in a room may help one attain inner peace, as it is said to calm the spirit and radiate love.

It is important that crystals be cleansed occasionally so that they can continue to resonate with the body and provide spiritual energy. You can do this by burying them in the earth overnight or placing them in salt water or in sea salt for 24 hours. I have a friend who buries hers in a flower pot filled with dry soil; she keeps it inside the house so she doesn't have to hunt for her crystals in the ground and then clean off the mud.

Vision Quests and Totems

Many tribes of American Indians participate in vision quests as a rite of passage into adulthood. There is a rigorous period of preparation before a vision quest; following this the participant goes out into nature for a time to seek a vision that is said to provide guidance for the rest of one's life. Natives would go out into the woods with no food or water, depriving themselves of basic needs for days until they experienced a vision.

Modern vision quests are similar to those of the Native Americans but are often less intense. Today, groups go out and prepare by meditating and fasting together; then individuals go out and spend time alone for a few hours or overnight.

During a time of individual questing, the participant may meet a totem that will remain with them to guide them through their lives. A totem is an animal, insect, or bird that you feel particularly close to. Perhaps a crow flew by the window while you were being born. This would be your totem. Possibly a cat ran in front of your path and prevented you from being hurt by something falling from a tree. A cat might then be your totem. A totem may appear in a dream or a vision. It may serve as a warning or could be sending a spiritual message. I have always had cats throughout my life and when I got my 3 new kittens a few years ago I felt protected...

The following are several common totems and the characteristics they represent:

Totem Type	**Characteristic**
Bear	Rebirth, Long Life
Pig	Prosperity, Spiritual Strength
Cat	Independence, Mystery
Coyote	Wisdom, Strength
Deer	Compassion, Peace
Dog	Loyalty, Protection
Eagle	Courage, Intelligence
Hawk	Intuition, Vision

Horse	Freedom, Stamina
Rabbit	Self-discipline, Grace
Snake	Impulsive, Transformation
Spider	Balance, Creativity
Turtle	Protection, Nurturing

I also feel an affinity towards the hawk. If I see a hawk, I am filled with the sense that everything will be all right. I'm not sure how the animal knows that I'm feeling down, but whenever I do, I just look into the sky and most the times I will find a hawk circling overhead to remind me that everything is going to be alright.

Discomfort

The Native American culture also believes that discomfort can bring about spiritual enlightenment. I am not suggesting that you go to the extremes some people pursue in order to become a spiritual person, but you may find some of the less dangerous types of discomfort helpful to you.

The Sun Dance, practiced by some Sioux Tribes, is probably the most well-known instance of pursuing spirituality through discomfort. Hooks or wood slats are inserted into piercings behind the back or chest muscles or into the shoulder muscles. Participants are then hoisted by leather straps; they remain hanging for a long period of time. The Mandan, Apache and Nez Pierce tribes have also been involved in similar suspension ceremonies that usually take place around the summer solstice. Sometimes these serve as the initiation for young men into warrior status.

It is thought that extreme pain brings about greater focus and can cause a trance state, leading to spiritual experiences of visions or other forms of enlightenment. This ceremony represents the death of the body and its spiritual awakening as the pain is removed. New freedom is often experienced as the hooks are removed and the participant is released. **Warning:** If you want to try this, do **not** attempt it without the guidance of an experienced practitioner. There are many other, less dangerous ways, to experience the discomfort that can lead to enlightenment.

Native American tribes have been practicing Sun Dance for centuries, even though the practice was outlawed for a time by the American government. This and other religious practices were again sanctioned through the 1978 passage of the American Indian Religious Freedom Act. For a very thorough description of this spiritual search, let me recommend the book The Crying for a Vision, by Walter Wangerin Jr. In his extensive Afterward, the author describes his participation in a Lakota Fire Dance, which shares many similarities to the Sun Dance described above.

Another Native American practice of discomfort is the sweat lodge. Of late, sweat lodge practices have been deemed highly dangerous, but this is mostly because people performed the ritual without really knowing what they were doing. Without an experienced expert to lead the practice it is possible to do great harm to participants.

In a sweat lodge ceremony, the body is subjected to high temperatures and extreme levels of humidity. Dehydration creates the discomfort which in turn may evoke visions and heightened spiritual awareness. The Lakota tribe is most well-known for using this practice, but other American Indian tribes across the United States and Canada have been known to also hold sweat lodges. When the body becomes distressed because of heat and water loss, the brain becomes distressed and is more focused as physical activity decreases.

Warning: Do **not** participate in a sweat lodge unless you have an experienced leader who is going to stay hydrated and watchful during the ritual. This is particularly dangerous to anyone with a major physical limitation. People with diabetes or heart disease should avoid this practice. Again, there are less dangerous ways to pursue enlightenment through discomfort, as many people have actually died doing this!

Perhaps the safest way to stimulate inner peace and heightened spirituality through discomfort is to fast. Many faiths have a long history of participation in this practice and, with certain modifications for specific physical conditions, fasting may be safely practiced by most individuals. The Mormons fast once a month. Some Christians fast during Lent; most commonly, Roman Catholics have been known to fast from eating meat other than fish on the Fridays leading up to Easter. Jews fast during Yom Kippur. Muslims fast between sunup and sundown during the month of Ramadan.

All of us fast without thinking of it. When we wake from sleep, our first meal is called – breakfast! No wonder it is considered the most important meal of the day; this meal is how we break the fast of the previous seven to eight hours in which our body has been cleansing itself of the toxins built up during the previous day. When we sleep, we fast from food and drink; we are just not aware of it, as we are when we consciously choose to fast.

Fasting usually consists of forgoing the intake of food and water for a short period of time, often starting at sundown. The simplest fasts extend for 12 to 24 hours, as exemplified by Yom Kippur fast. Other fasts may be conducted across a longer span of time. The Ramadan fast lasts, with certain limitations and exemptions, for an entire month. The Jewish Talmud gives examples of individuals who fasted for longer periods.

A 40-day fast is the most extreme. It usually consists of fasting from everything except water. The interesting part of this fast is that in the first few days of this fast, the body first cleanses itself of toxins; after that, body fat begins to be burned. By the 40th day, all excess body fat has been consumed. On this day the individual – who for the past couple weeks has been relatively free from hunger – begins to experience serious hunger pangs again. If the fast is continued past this point, the body begins to consume muscle tissue, which marks the beginning of starvation. For obvious reasons, extreme fasting is **not** recommended for diabetics or others with physical conditions that would become life-threatening if regular nourishment were suspended. Any extended fast should only be pursued after it is cleared by your personal physician.

There are well-known benefits to regular fasting in moderation. In the process of removing toxins from the physical body, fasting also raises spiritual awareness. You do not need to fast for an extended time either, in order to experience these benefits. Even a 24-hour fast is long enough for you to become much more keenly aware of your spiritual being. Praying and meditation are common activities while fasting; in addition to providing easier focus on spiritual things, these activities also help distract you from your hunger!

It is possible for diabetics and others with restrictive physical conditions to experience the benefits of a partial fast, but I stress, this should not be even considered without extensive discussion with your doctor. I have known diabetics who, with their physician's blessing, were able to maintain healthy blood sugar levels while fasting for a single meal or even abstaining for 24 hours from food, all the while maintaining a medically modified liquid diet prescribed by their doctor.

Interestingly enough, even a slightly modified diet can allow one to experience the spiritual benefits present in a complete fast. I am convinced that many of these benefits are triggered by the conscious choice of the practitioner to put aside normal eating practices in exchange for time spent in pursuit of God.

Chapter 6: Thoughtful Actions – Meditation, Affirmation, and Prayer

Meditation is a vehicle to achieve inner peace and has been known as such since ancient times. Prayer is a communication with your Source; prayer can range from the simple, one-word "Help!" to a short prayer before (and after, if you are a Muslim) meals thanking God for the food, to an intense conversation with your maker. Affirmations are a form of positive self-talk.

Technique # 19 – Perform Affirmations

Affirmations are an uplifting way to feed your spirit and may be considered a form of meditation. For example, in transcendental meditation, the guru gives the person meditating a mantra or statement to be repeated; this often is a sort of positive affirmation.

Affirmations help replace your internal negative dialogue with a positive alternative. They can carry you a long ways toward being at peace with yourself and the world around you.

Affirmations are a little easier than what I will call full-blown meditation. They consist of a single phrase or sentence. Affirmations can be spoken anywhere; you can repeat them at your desk, in the shower as part of your morning ritual, or wherever you are. You don't have to sit or stand; you can take any position you like. Your physical posture is completely irrelevant when it comes to affirmations. They don't even require much concentration. You can easily recite them as you drive to work, take a walk, etc.

Affirmations are worded as positive statements. They are realities you have chosen to affirm or truth statements you have selected to guide your life. The affirmation, "I release all my fears and trust in my higher power to protect me" is a guiding statement. It is a promise to yourself that you will not fear the unknown. It also states your confidence that you will be protected and your needs will be taken care of by a force outside of yourself.

Affirmations can carry you a long ways toward inner peace. They are a tool with which to replace negative and destructive thoughts and attitudes with beliefs that build and nourish your life. The statement of affirmation is a beneficial form of "brainwashing." The idea behind it is that the more often you speak something, the more it becomes real to you. There is nothing wrong with this kind of brainwashing if it helps you become a better person. Here are some affirmations you might find useful in your own life:

- My Source will supply all my needs.
- I am a spiritual being housed in a physical body.
- I can love myself when I make mistakes.

- I accept each part of myself without judging.
- As I accept myself, so I accept other people, without condemnation.
- I give my love without conditions, expecting nothing in return.
- God's love flows through me and outward toward others.
- I am loving, forgiving, and kind.
- I look for beauty around me.
- I choose to do the right and good thing.
- I see the magic and the miracle in life.
- I have all I need.
- I am growing spiritually.
- I do what I can to ease the troubles of others.
- I acknowledge that there is good in all people, including myself.

I suggest you write your chosen affirmations on index cards. Small 3 by 5 inch index cards easily slide into your pocket or your purse for easy access. Take them with you and pull them out for repetition periodically throughout the day. You can also glue a magnetic strip to the back of a card and stick it to your refrigerator at home or a file cabinet at work. Several times during the day, take a look at your affirmations and speak them out loud if at all possible. Before long, the concepts become part of your life. You will become what your affirmations suggest, as they become part of your subconscious.

Technique #20 – Meditation

Meditation has been linked with spirituality for centuries. Meditation is a means of opening the mind to inner peace.

Many types of meditations exist. You can try most of them by yourself, although some types require personal instruction from a teacher.

J. Krishnamurti, an Indian philosopher and spiritualist, wrote, "Meditation is not a means to an end. It is both the means *and* the end." One effect of meditation is that of calming the whole person. As it brings stillness, it can actually initiate healing and improve physical and emotional health. Meditation may help you focus on daily tasks and it is able to increase your effectiveness, both at work and at home. If you are frequently called on to make major decisions, you may also benefit; meditation is known to help a person detach emotionally from a situation in order to think clearly and discern the best path to follow. Meditation also promotes unwavering focus, which can help keep distractions from derailing your purpose.

In meditation, you experience silence. This includes quieting the inner voice, which is always clamoring for attention. This may not be easy to do at first. You don't just sit down and decide to meditate for 30 minutes unless you've been practicing this and building up to it. As you begin, don't be surprised if you find yourself drifting off into daydreams, falling asleep, or becoming distracted by frustration if you don't succeed in the first couple minutes. Meditation is a skill; as such, it can be learned. All you need is repeated practice over time. Meditation is difficult at first, but it will be well worth the work. An easy way to start meditating can be found in AudioEntertainment's YouTube Video "A Beginner's Guide to Meditation~Learn To Meditate in 5 Easy Steps.

Once you get the hang of meditation, you may find yourself calmer and less likely to get angry. In meditation, all bodily functions slow down while your energy increases. Everything from blood flow to breathing becomes slower, until you have reached a sort of balance. I know one person who is able to relax her entire body when meditating. Her pulse decreases to single digits and if you were to raise her arm above her head and let go, it would fall limply to her side.

In meditation, the spirit becomes freer; peacefulness takes over. You can receive communication from spiritual sources, when in meditation. The calm that occurs during meditation is something you can actually carry with you into other life situations.

One common type of meditation, made famous during the 1960s and '70s by celebrities, including the Beatles, is called Transcendental Meditation. This is an intense form of meditation, patterned after the Hindu practice of Vedanta meditation. In Transcendental Meditation, the practitioner sits comfortably and clears the mind of all chatter and clutter by repeating a mantra given by a guru. This mantra may be something as simple as "I am strong, powerful and compassionate". The lotus position is the posture most suited to this type of meditation because it can be maintained a long period of time without too much discomfort.

Zen or Zazen Meditation is a popular form that uses a koan, or a phrase focusing upon a riddle with no real answer. The theory behind this type of meditation is that the mind will overwhelm itself and stop thinking altogether when an answer cannot be achieved. The result is total silence. This mediation requires the body to sit in a totally *un*comfortable position. You sit with your spine straight and your back completely unsupported. After a while the body begins to ache. You are expected to stay in this position without thinking as you pass through the pain onto the other side.

Mindful Meditation is a bit easier and is popular today. Vipassana is the Buddhist meditation practice from which this form is derived. In Mindful Meditation, you focus on being fully present, whether you are on a bus going home or in your bedroom. The mind is allowed to wander freely and you observe, without judgment, whatever thoughts surface. The idea here is that the mind will eventually calm itself and will quiet down.

Walking meditation occurs when you walk and focus on your walking. This type of meditation is sometimes done in a labyrinth, but you can walk anywhere: along a path, on a sidewalk, around a track or in a parking lot. When the body is in motion it is easier to focus on what it is doing. You focus on what each part of your body does to impel you forward.

Other, more difficult forms of meditation include Qigong, a healing form of meditation with roots in the martial arts and Kundalini yoga, which has a profound religious underpinning dealing with chakras and the coiling snake of the spine.

Think of meditation as a way to let off steam from everyday life. Use it as a tool to calm the mind while increasing your spiritual awareness. Meditation can help you think clearly, move more deliberately and live more calmly.

Technique # 21 – Foster a Relationship with Your Higher Power; Pray

Do you worship God, Jesus, Allah, Buddha or another Ultimate Source? I encourage you to pursue this connection through prayer.

Philip James Bailey, an English poet said, "Prayer is the spirit speaking truth to truth." Ralph Waldo Emerson, American transcendentalist said, "No man ever prayed heartily without learning something." Both of these quotes are very true.

Think about your Source frequently. Pray frequently. Keep open channels and maintain a running conversation with God. Nothing helps more than to have someone on whom you can unload all your worries and fears. At the same time, your joy is increased as you express gratitude toward your Source when things go well. Your prayers may feel one-sided at times, but your Maker hears. Your Source may answer in a way you do not anticipate, so keep your mind and your eyes open.

Maybe you speak regularly to your guardian angel or to your deceased grandmother. This line of communication is important to some spiritual people; they consider it essential to keep these lines of communication open every day.

Many of us are taught to pray to God every night. I find myself praying several times a day. I pray for safety while driving on an icy road or when I need a little more money in order to pay my bills. I pray for others who are suffering difficulties. I pray just to give thanks for what I have and for experiencing a great day. I pray for forgiveness when I do something wrong or I pray just to share with God something really great that he provided for me that day.

Of course, your prayer does not need to be a memorized text. Prayer is, by definition, the outpouring of your heart to your Source. It may be considered a form of meditation, because you focus your mind on a single activity, communicating with the divine. No other thoughts come into play except for speaking to your Source.

Memorized prayers do have a purpose. Most Christians know the Lord's Prayer and Catholics repeat the prayers with their rosary beads. Some Jewish traditions have prayers for every activity of the day. Pre-formulated prayers can help you focus on the presence of God; they may serve as a precursor to prayer spoken in your own words from your own heart.

If you need help getting started, here are a few suggestions that may aid you:

1. Sit, stand or kneel comfortably. Do not lie down as it is too easy to fall asleep.

2. Review your day, looking for the good things you were given. Thank your Source for all the good things he brought into your life. Thank God if you had enough food to eat, found enough money to pay the bills, or were hugged by a family member.

3. Pray for others in need. Pray for friends who are struggling financially. Ask God to help friends who are sick.

4. Ask for things you need. Pray for that bill you don't know how you'll pay, for the strength to love someone who is difficult to love, for patience with your children.

5. Ask forgiveness for ways in which you have wronged others or dishonored your Source.

6. Complete your prayer by thanking your Source for listening to you and for responding to your requests.

There is no right or wrong way to pray. What is important is that the line of communication is open. Some people just start talking to their Source as if they were speaking to a friend. Others are more formal about the whole affair. It really doesn't matter how you do this; your relationship with your Source is the primary aspect of your spiritual life. Praying fosters an awareness that you are not alone, that your needs are heard and that your prayers can be answered.

Technique #22 – Find or Start a Group

Pursuing spiritual maturity and inner peace is often easier when you can share the pursuit with others. We all need friends in which we can confide, with whom we can commiserate, and with whom to share both our joys and sorrows.

One way to find people who can share our spiritual quest is to look for a church, synagogue, mosque or other group. Don't be too quick to become a member; you do not have to 'join' a church to be involved in one. Visit several groups to see which one is right for you. Do you feel comfortable there? Are you treated kindly and with respect? Do the members seem to be the kind of people you want to learn from or emulate? Do the other members invite you to join in with them in discussions and other activities? Are you comfortable with the practices and theories of the organization? Can you see yourself with this group several years down the road?

It is important to feel comfortable with a group of people because you will share the intimacies of spiritual life with them. If the people do not welcome you, if they do not make it a point to include you as a newcomer and take you under their wing, you may find it difficult to open yourself up with them. If you don't agree with the theology of a group, you may find it impossible to grow spiritually there. A Wiccan or Pagan practitioner might be very spiritual, but they would find it difficult to join in a Christian group. If you are a Christian, but you have a hard time wrapping your head around the trinity being three in one person, you may want to find a church that can adequately explain it to you before you can go forward with them.

There are many community groups that promote spirituality but do not have a priest, minister, rabbi or other religious official in charge. Here are a few:

- Kiwanis is a group of local people who help the homeless, sick, and people affected by natural disasters. They feed the hungry and are instrumental in several charities.

- The Lions Club performs many humanitarian services in almost every corner of the United States and abroad.

- Goodwill relies on volunteers and donations to help millions of people throughout the world. In most cases, money generated by local thrift stores stays within the community.

- The American Red Cross provides comfort and support for those in need, especially in disaster situations.

Check locally for other organizations that use volunteers to provide humanitarian services to others. Most cities have a 411 number you can call to learn about volunteering opportunities in your area.

Look for spiritual support groups. You aren't the only one out there trying to grow spiritually. If you can't find a group, start one. A public library or a local church or school may be willing to provide a meeting place. You can also start a group on-line. Share what you have learned about spirituality and inner peace while finding out how others became more in tune with their spirit and learning what they have done to grow spiritually.

Technique #23 – Find a Teacher

You can learn a lot about different things from books and videos, but sometimes what you read will not hit home until you have someone to teach you. Seek a teacher who is a priest or pastor. If you opt for a New Age approach, seek out a Reiki Master or another type of practitioner. Another option is to learn from a yoga instructor or a Tai Chi Master. Look for a mentor who most exemplifies the type of spirituality you wish to build.

A friend of mine grew up in a white community, but his mother was full-blooded Cherokee. He felt drawn to the Cherokee way and sought out a Cherokee elder to be his mentor. Since Native American spirituality is largely taught by rote, learning from a mentor worked much better than reading books about Cherokee culture. His mentor taught him many things, from the ways of the medicine wheel to the dance and the drum circle. My friend found his totem and now uses it to aid him in everyday life. He grew to be in tune with Nature and his surroundings. Today he runs a successful business and has a thriving personal life, all because an old man chose to share his Native American wisdom with a young seeker.

Another friend has always felt drawn to crystals. She could feel their vibrations in ways I never could. She sought out a crystal healer to teach her how to use the stones to improve both her own well-being and that of others. Her skills grew by leaps and bounds once she had a teacher. Prior to that, she knew all the properties of the different stones, but without a teacher, she didn't know what to do with them.

It can be a daunting task to find a mentor/teacher who can help you grow spiritually. A priest or minister may willingly help you grow in your faith, but many other teachers require you to prove yourself to them before they will take you under their wing. The best way to go about obtaining a mentor is to be as open and honest with them as you can. If you know nothing about Native American spirituality and you want help from an elder, you may experience difficulty, especially if you are not Native American in the first place. Many teachers, especially American Indians, hold their spirituality close to their heart and do not share it willingly. An elder may require you to study the tribe on your own before they will take you on as a student.

Be careful to choose a teacher or mentor who takes teaching seriously and is secure enough in themselves that they will not become jealous if you surpass them. Sadly, there are people out there who prey on innocent seekers. If someone asks you for money, I would be very cautious. I can understand charging for learning materials, but charging exorbitant fees for time spent should be considered cautiously. Find out if others have used this person as a mentor and see what they think of him or her. A good teacher will only take on a few students; they will become personally involved in fostering a friendship that can last a lifetime. A wonderful example of a mentoring relationship can be found in the book, <u>Tuesdays With Morrie</u>, by Mitch Albom.

Alcoholics Anonymous has the right idea when it comes to a mentor or teacher. Each member is assigned a more mature sponsor who takes them under wing and shows them the ropes. If a member experiences cravings and is tempted to drink, his sponsor is available at moment's notice to help him through the crisis. The sponsor is not paid for this service, but is 'paying it forward', since another person has done the same for him in the past.

A mentoring relationship can last a few weeks or a lifetime. The mentor teaches by example and nurtures the student until the student has achieved a chosen objective. When it comes to spirituality and inner peace, there is always something new to learn. Whether your teacher is a wise man or woman, a healer, your Aunt Sally or a friend, it is important to maintain this relationship. Who knows? You may be able to pay it forward yourself someday by mentoring someone else.

Chapter 7: Final Stages – Surrender and Patience

Two final aspects of pursuing spirituality and inner peace are surrender and patience. This is the time for your ego to surrender ultimate control to your Source. Surrender is the "Do-what-you-will-with-me" stage while patience adds to the mix a willingness to wait as long as it takes for your Source to set things right.

Technique #24 – Surrender

Many people feel they should be in control at all times. They control their kids and their partner. They control coworkers, or try to, and they control their lives and each situation that arises. To these people, the word "surrender" feels like losing control, but that could not be farther from the truth.

Surrendering to your Source does not mean a complete loss of control. Surrender is not a matter of acknowledging the randomness of Fate. Rather it consists of acknowledging that in reality you are not in control in the first place. The scariest part is admitting how puny you are.

Control is largely a myth. Things happen all around you that you have no control over. You couldn't even control where you were born. What makes you think you can control your circumstances now? The good news is that there is a Source who *is* in control. As crazy as this world seems, you have a Source who – so far – has managed to keep you alive, probably allowing you to thrive in the process. It is that Source to whom you are being asked to entrust yourself.

After you have surrendered, you come to understand that even the bad things that happen to you have a purpose. You can't see what is around the corner, (unless, of course, you are a psychic). A string of bad luck may be coming your way, but what you choose to do during that time can both define you and set you on a completely different course toward the future. Some circumstances you cannot change, but you still have the power to choose your responses and your attitudes toward them.

Surrender means that you take whatever comes, good or bad, and find a way to deal with it. Based upon your confidence in your Source, you take in the experience, digest whatever you can learn from it, and spit it out to the best of your ability.

I have a friend who spent most of her life trying to control her children. One child became a drug addict. She spent much of her energy taking this child to psychologists, psychiatrists and treatment centers, but the kid always got out and started using drugs again. Even after he turned 18 and she really had no authority to control his actions, this mother felt responsible for his life. One day, her husband sat her down and explained that her actions were only making matters worse. Her child was intent on doing drugs regardless of her intent to stop him. He urged her to quit trying to control her son, letting go of him and trusting that God is even more capable of caring for him than she is. My friend chose to let go and place her son in God's hands. She realized she could do nothing but provide an example and offer advice to her son when he was open to receive it.

Shortly after she let go, the son overdosed, but that overdose probably saved his life. After nearly dying, he finally realized how dangerous the drugs were and took initiative to quit. Because his mom surrendered the situation to God, her son is now in recovery. Today he has a job and a wife with a baby on the way. Surrender helped this young man and probably saved the sanity of his mother.

Another friend lost his job when the company he worked for closed its doors. Three weeks later his wife was laid off from her job. Then the car broke down, but he had no resources to get it fixed.

There was no way my friend could control his circumstances. At first he was angry and didn't even try to pursue new jobs. However, after a few weeks he decided it was not worth all the energy it took to worry about things he could not change. As his first act of living in the moment, my friend decided to walk to the grocery store to get a few meager supplies. It was raining, but he went anyway.

A man who lived a few doors down the street was driving past and, recognizing his neighbor, stopped to offer him a ride. My friend gratefully accepted the offer, explaining that his car had broken down after he lost his job and he hadn't been able to fix it. The neighbor asked where he used to work. The man replied that he had been an accountant for a grocery store. As it turned out, the neighbor supervised a dollar store chain and just "happened" to be looking to hire an accountant. Not only did my friend land a job that day, but his wife also began working there.

You may call this fate or chance, but my friend did not have any intention of leaving the house until he had surrendered to the situation and decided to go on with his life no matter what. If he hadn't "given up" and if he had not accepted that ride, he would most likely be homeless today.

Surrender isn't a lack of control; it is more like setting yourself free. You free yourself from worry and go with the flow of life, trusting your Source to carry you along. Surrender allows you to view your surroundings more objectively; you are no longer restrained by the fear of trying hard to get nowhere.

Surrender to your Source means you put all your trust there. You may know some bad times, but what you learn from them makes you a stronger, wiser person. You no longer have expectations for what will happen to you, so you take what life hands out and are grateful. See what Burt Harding says about surrender in the YouTube video, The Meaning of Surrender. He gives a good explanation of the process.

Surrender, opening up to your Source and resting there, can bring increased peace and harmony into your life.

Technique #25 – Have Patience

Rome wasn't built in a day, or so the saying goes. You are not going to become a spiritual giant overnight. It takes time and practice to grow spiritually. Changes that are made purposefully and slowly tend to stick in the brain better and become a habit, so, I'm sorry to have to inform you, there is no incantation, prayer or wave of a wand that will make change happen quickly in most cases.

The problem with the time it takes to change, is that some people get bored and lose interest. It takes about 21-30 days of doing something repeatedly to change a habit. If you are trying to stop snacking at night before bedtime, your body is going to crave food at night until you have stubbornly resisted nighttime eating for about 30 days. Of course, this can be facilitated by taking in proper nutrition during the daytime. Once the 30 days is over, however, your body will basically accept that it isn't going to get food at bedtime anymore. Strengthening your spirit is not just a matter of changing a single habit; it consists of changing an entire lifetime of learned patterns. Consequently, you cannot expect to find inner peace in 30 days. It might take a year or five years, but most likely you will be working on this for the rest of your life. The good news is, as long as you are working toward that objective, you will continue to grow spiritually.

In your pursuit of spiritual growth, let me encourage you to sit back and enjoy the ride. Don't take your pursuit too seriously, but relax and have some fun along the way. So what if you skip a day of affirmations! You can always pick up this discipline again the next day. Remember to live in the moment and to smell the roses every chance you get!

Conclusion

I hope this book has helped you to know what you can do in order to grow spiritually. Heaven knows, we need more spiritually mature people on this earth. The world can be a frightening place; it's the spiritual ones who shine the light of hope on people living in the darkness, showing them the way out of the dungeon of despair. As you grow spiritually, may notice that you have an increasing positive impact on the lives of other people.

Your next step, as you start the process of growing spiritually, is to try some of the techniques in this book. Do not get discouraged if you see no change at first; remember it may take considerable time before you see progress. Take baby steps into the world of spiritual development. Pretty soon you will be able to say, "I am growing in spirit, I am learning peace, and I am vitally connected to my Source."

It is important that you do things at your own pace. Most of the techniques to increase spirituality and inner peace presented in this book are easy to do, but if you struggle with some of them, it is better to skip them for now. Try the technique again at another time or skip it all together. It is much more important that you 'make haste slowly' so as to retain what you need in order to grow spiritually.

Be sure to choose your top three techniques from this book and focus on them for the next month. Once you have made them a habit, choose 3 more things from this book that you think would benefit you the most. Practice makes perfect! I wish you the best of luck on your spiritual journey and I hope that you live happily ever after!

Finally, if you discovered at least one thing that has helped you or that you think would be beneficial to someone else, be sure to take a few seconds to easily post a quick positive review. As an author, your positive feedback is desperately needed. Your highly valuable five star reviews are like a river of golden joy flowing through a sunny forest of mighty trees and beautiful flowers! *To do your good deed in making the world a better place by helping others with your valuable insight, just leave a nice review.*

My Other Books and Audio Books
www.AcesEbooks.com

Peak Performance Books

Health Books

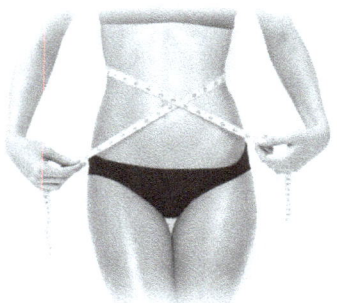

Be sure to check out my audio books as well!

Check out my website at: **www.AcesEbooks.com** for a complete list of all of my books and high quality audio books. I enjoy bringing you the best knowledge in the world and wish you the best in using this information to make your journey through life better and more enjoyable! **Best of luck to you!**

www.ingramcontent.com/pod-product-compliance
Lightning Source LLC
Chambersburg PA
CBHW051425070526
44584CB00023B/3578